I'm Saved...What's Next?

Building a Relationship - 10 Keys to Walking with God

BRENDA R. ROBY

WESTBOW
PRESS®
A DIVISION OF THOMAS NELSON
& ZONDERVAN

WestBow Press books may be ordered through booksellers or by contacting:

WestBow Press
A Division of Thomas Nelson & Zondervan
1663 Liberty Drive
Bloomington, IN 47403
www.westbowpress.com
844-714-3454

ISBN: 978-1-5127-5655-5 (sc)
ISBN: 978-1-5127-5704-0 (e)

Library of Congress Control Number: 2016915330

Print information available on the last page.

WestBow Press rev. date: 08/10/2021

Father,

I just want to say thank You for all You have done for me. You have given me another chance to partner with You to bless Your people. Father, You never gave up on me when I backed away from previous projects, and for that I am forever grateful! You are truly faithful and worthy to be praised! May this book minister to the hearts and lives of Your people and accomplish all that You desire in Jesus's name.

Love you always,
Brenda

Dedication

I would like to dedicate this book to my pastors, both past and present, who have shaped my future with the word of God. Thanks for preaching and teaching the unadulterated, uncompromised word of God with clarity, accuracy, and boldness.

To my present pastor, Dr. Gloria Williams. You have been an example of Psalm 37:37, "Mark the perfect man, and behold the upright: for the end of that man is peace." I watch how you handle yourself in situations, and you remain the same. You walk out the word in your life, and you are an example of what His word can do. Because of this transparency, I am able to receive and apply what I've learned to my life and experience His promises firsthand. Thank you for being a great leader and a great example for me to follow. God bless you!

Acknowledgements

My most sincere and humble thanks goes to all who encouraged me along this journey. Thank you for supporting me when I stepped out on faith to pursue God's vision. We did it!

To the WestBow Press staff, thank you for your assistance in the publishing process. You guided me through each stage to bring God's vision to fruition. I am grateful.

To my mother, Mattie Richardson. Mom, your character and integrity are what caused me to desire to be like you. I noticed long ago how you handled yourself in ways that were peaceful and kind. Another thing I noticed was the fact that people genuinely wanted to be around you and loved you dearly. You are everyone's auntie Mattie. I didn't know it then, but I now know that it was because you allowed Jesus to lead you. All the time you had been walking by the Spirit. I am the woman I am today because of you. Thanks for being a Proverbs 31 woman, for we rise up and call you blessed!

To Anthony, my wonderful husband and best friend, I acknowledge you. You have always been there for me, supporting me in every one of my God-driven endeavors. You hear God and follow quickly thereafter, causing our family to be blessed. Thanks so very much for being a dedicated husband, father, and friend. I love you.

To Natazsa and Marc-Anthony, my precious babies. You have grown into awesome and productive young adults. Thanks for allowing me to constantly pour the wisdom of God into you and you receive it. You are the best children that any mom could ever desire, and I am blessed that God gave you to me. Continue progressing in the things of God, for He is directing you into your purpose.

To Minda, my teacher-cousin, thanks for assisting me with the initial review of this book. You are such a sweet, caring, and blessed woman of God. I appreciate the time and effort you put into *I'm Saved ... What's Next?* I speak blessings over your family and all you put your hands to.

To my entire family, I cannot truly express into words how your love, prayers, and encouragement along this journey have strengthened me. Thanks for always asking, "How's the book coming along?" This gave me the inspiration to continue pressing forward. May God bless each of you is my prayer.

Contents

Preface 1

Introduction 3

Religion or Relationship? 5

What Is a Relationship? 7

Key 1 (Love) 9

Key 2 (Trust) 15

Key 3 (Agree) 21

Key 4 (Devote) 25

Key 5 (Submit) 29

Key 6 (Humble) 33

Key 7 (Ask Every Day) 39

Key 8 (Meditation and Application) 43

Key 9 (Walk by the Spirit) 47

Key 10 (Be Persistent) 49

Just Doing Church 51

Revelation from God 57

On Your Way 61

Decision to Receive God's Forgiveness 65

Encouragement Just for You 67

Preface

Thank you for opening *I'm Saved ... What's Next?* to view its content. This book was given to me by the unction of Holy Spirit. Often I was awakened to write, and sometimes throughout the day I would just be prompted. I began keeping paper and pens on my nightstand ... prepared for the task. I pray all the time for salvation because I'm believing God for family, friends, neighbors and all who are not saved to receive His gift. I just believe God for all to hear the message and receive Jesus as Savior and Lord of their lives.

I once was challenged with not knowing what to do next after receiving salvation. I now know that the next step is to begin building a relationship with God. There is so much for us to learn, but as we desire to get to know Him, He shows us how to walk out our new life in Christ.

In the beginning of my writing, I thought this was going to be directed to those newly saved. Unfortunately, that was my thought and not God's. I'm learning that God's vision is vaster than ours. He doesn't want to leave anyone out. His heart is for all to grow closer to Him. As I began to delve more into the heart of the book, I noticed that I was experiencing having to walk out many of the topics that I was writing about. It's funny, but I had to refer to the writing and make sure I was doing things God's way. I had situations that arose causing me to agree with God even when I didn't want to. I had to submit myself to His mission because I knew that if I didn't, I would not be pleasing Him and I would not get the blessings I truly desired.

This book is for everyone! It's for those who are recently saved, who have been saved a while, or who need to come/return to Christ. The ten keys listed are what God instructs us to operate in daily so we can build a relationship with Him. While honoring God and displaying His character in the earth, men will see Him in us, and we will have the opportunity to touch their lives with hope. It's all about us being made better because we choose to do things God's way, consequently making others around us better. *I'm Saved … What's Next?* was written to be a blessing to your life. Open your heart and follow God's word, and see how He will reveal His plan to you day by day. It's not by your might, nor by your power, but by His Spirit will you be able to accomplish supernatural deeds in the earth. You can do all things (what He's called you to do) through Christ who strengthens you. So let's journey with Jesus and leave our ways of doing things *behind* so we can *move forward* and truly build a relationship with Christ. You can do it!

Introduction

Welcome—you have now become a member of God's family! We are so happy that you have made a choice to live for God. It is a choice, and it's the best one you could ever have made, glory to God! Jesus loves you so much, and for you to accept what He has done for you personally makes all of what He went through worth it. You know, He would leave the ninety-nine sheep just for one. You are that special one that He was after, and He longed for you so He kept after you until you said *yes.*

I remember when I first got saved; I tried so hard to be saved. What was it, and how was I supposed to act? All I knew was I wanted to please God but was not sure how. You may be feeling the same way. Well, after many trials and errors—after many times feeling defeated—I've learned that it's simple—take it one day at a time. Read God's word daily, and meditate on it (think about what you have read throughout the day). Ask God to open up the word to you so you can have clarity. Ask Him to reveal Himself to you. In order to build a relationship with anyone, you must spend time with him or her to learn his or her voice and ways.

Relationships take time to be established, so do not get frustrated. People often wonder how to hear from God … just stay in His word. There are keys that I have listed in this book that will assist you in creating a foundation for building a relationship with God that will last. As you begin agreeing with God, humbling yourself, showing devotion to Him and being persistent in building a relationship with God, you will begin to hear better from God. As you seek God more, the Holy Spirit will begin to reveal the secret things of God to you. After a while, you will get the hang of hearing; you will learn when it is *Him* who's speaking to you.

I remember when I began to truly hear from God. I heard something in my "knower." I said to myself, *This must be God because I could not have come up with something so simple, yet so deep!* It's going to be an aha moment for you.

You have received God's gift, Jesus Christ, because you came to a realization that you needed a Savior. This is a good place to be. We all had to receive this revelation. Now, here is how to begin walking out your new life in Christ. You must show God that you love Him. Love is an action word; therefore, you must show Him your love, not just tell Him. You do it by walking out His word daily (allowing the word of God to be final authority or the measurement of standard in your life). By this you are showing Him that you *choose* to live your life His way, by His principles—no matter what. In actuality, once you received Jesus as your personal Lord and Savior, your life now belongs to God. The way you used to live has to die, and you now purpose to live your new life in Christ. You start building a relationship with Him by getting into a good Bible-based church that teaches the pure, unadulterated, uncompromised word of God, that shares the love of God with others, that worships God and is determined to teaching its members how to live like Christ, and that reaches out to help those in need.

A healthy relationship allows both partners to feel appreciated. God appreciates it when you hunger and thirst (desire) after righteousness—doing things the right way … His way. He knows you are new at this and you will falter sometimes. Our Father appreciates your effort in striving to put defeat and fear out of your way and pressing continuously toward Him.

At one point in time, you didn't have anyone who would always go to battle for you, but now you do. Do you realize that every sin you could possibly do has already been forgiven by Jesus? God loves you so very much, and He goes into this relationship already being the giver. Just trust Him. Show your appreciation for what He's already done for you by following His word, learning His principles, and letting your lifestyle be an example for others to live by. As you stand on His word, He is faithful to perform it in your life. Our Father has a plan for your life, and it is good! So let's begin building a relationship with God today … you can do it!

Religion or Relationship?

The word *religion* stirs up negative feelings in people. In and of itself, it is not bad. The definition according to Webster's is an organized system of beliefs, ceremonies, and rules used to worship a god or a group of gods. In other words, it is a category to place your faith in. We are Christians; therefore, our religion is Christianity. Now, the word *religion* becomes negative when it is in its adjective form. When a person becomes religious, doing works that he or she thinks will get him or her into heaven or appease God and it's not what God wants, then all of the works are considered religious.

Christianity is not about being religious; rather, it is about building a relationship with Christ. You are not getting into heaven by the works that you do—no matter how great—but by what you receive. Jesus has already done the works; all you and I must do is believe. We must believe that God is the Sovereign One and that He sent Jesus, His only Son, to die in our stead; we must believe that He was raised from the dead and is now seated at the right hand of His Father (God). We must then work out our salvation with fear and trembling. This means that we must rise each day with the intention and determination to please God. We are walking in the "new" life that we've been given through Jesus Christ. Everything we are learning and every scripture that we read, we are to put into demonstration in our actions, discussion, and character. This assists us in building our personal relationship with the Lord.

> *Christianity is not about being religious; rather, it is about building a relationship with Christ.*

What Is a Relationship?

Come unto me, all ye that labour and are heavy laden, and I will give you rest. Take my yoke upon you, and learn of me; for I am meek and lowly in heart: and ye shall find rest unto your souls. (Matthew 11:28–29)

A relationship is a bond or a rapport with someone. Here is a quote from an unknown author: "Good relationships don't just happen; they take time, patience, and two people who truly want to be together." God's relationship to you is not based on your merit (value, worthiness, goodness) but on His unconditional love and Jesus's merit. In the scripture above, Jesus is saying to take His teachings and learn more about Him. He wants to give you peace in the midst of whatever you may be facing each day. He's entreating you to enter into a relationship with Him and explaining what you'll receive from this union. As you come to Him and submit to His teachings, you will find rest, victory, and success in this life. A relationship with our Lord and Savior is going to require work on your part, so make time. The more time spent, the better the relationship. The better the relationship, the more trust you will have in God. It does not happen overnight, but with sacrifice and patience, you will have a relationship better than you could have ever imagined.

> *Loving God's way will sensitize you to the needs of others.*

Through building your relationship with our Father (vertically), you can now begin to build or rebuild relationships laterally (spouse, family, friends, business partners, etc.). Building a strong, secure, and loving spiritual relationship with the Almighty God is the foundation you need to create well-established relationships in the physical world. If you cannot love, trust, and agree with God and follow His plan, then it will be very difficult for you to truly love someone in your life. Loving God's way will sensitize you to the needs of others, causing you to be more proactive rather than reactive in situations.

Key #1

Love

Love never fails. (1 Corinthians 13:8)

It is amazing once you read the entire chapter of 1 Corinthians 13—you'll discover that everything passes away except for love. "Love never fails" means that love never dies, it never gives up, and it never becomes obsolete or goes out of style. This is why love is so vitally important to our walk with Christ.

In building any relationship, you must have love, especially when building one with the almighty God. There are at least four types of love described in the Greek language:

- *agape*—unconditional
- *eros*—romance
- *philia*—friendship
- *storge*—natural affection (family)

The greatest of these is *agape* (the way God loves) because it is self-sufficient. It does not require any aid, support, or interaction for survival. When you love how God loves, then you simply love because you care. There are no conditions, only your willingness. You just do it because it is the *right*eous thing to do. The others depend on people, situations, or circumstances to be favorable in order for them to stay intact. They are conditional and are based on our feelings and emotions, which can change in an instant due to hurt, disappointment, or rejection.

God is love, and those who love Him must love Him with all their heart, soul, mind, and strength. The next thing you must do is love your neighbor (those you come in contact with) as yourself. It means to love others by being kind, whether or not they deserve it. Treat them how you *would like* for them to treat you—not necessarily how they *are* treating you!

There is an old adage that says, "What goes around comes around." Many people (including Christians) refer to this act as karma, but let's digress for just a moment. We as believers need to understand the original meaning of karma before we are so quick to associate our lives and things happening in them with this term. I researched it and discovered that karma is a concept of the Buddhist and Hindu religions, and it means that you get what you give, which is similar to the scripture, "For whatsoever a man soweth; that shall he also reap" (Galatians 6:7). Unlike this scripture, karma is referring to the afterlife or reincarnation. As Christians, this is not our philosophy. We are not reincarnated and do not get a second chance to relive this life in another body and try to do better next time. No, God gives us one chance and that's it.

Hebrews 9:27 says, "And as it is appointed unto men once to die, but after this the judgment." Once we leave this earthen vessel (the body), there's judgment. And our receiving or neglecting Christ will determine our future—eternal life in heaven with Jesus or eternal suffering in hell. Karma is based on your works, but grace is based on your faith. The apostle Paul summed it up in Ephesians 2:8–9: "For by grace are ye saved through faith; and that not of yourselves: it is the gift of God: Not of works, lest any man should boast." Our Father has given us a way out of our mess. We may have done wrong, but to receive Jesus as our Savior and Lord, we are now able to live our lives according to His word. We now have eternal life in Christ Jesus—that's good news!

Now, let's return to our original train of thought. The cliché of what goes around comes around refers to the idea that what you give out will one day come knocking on your door. When it arrives, ask yourself, "Is this what I want?" If not, then begin observing the way you talk to and treat others, and then make changes in your love walk so you will begin to get the results you truly desire. In building your love walk with God, you must respect, honor, cherish, and obey Him.

- **Respect**—honoring God by acting the way He deems appropriate. The way we do this is to do what's right because it is right, and do it with the right heart, attitude, and motive. We conduct ourselves in ways that are pleasing before Him (telling the truth, speaking what God says and not what we think or how we feel, and obeying His word).

- **Honor**—recognizing the value of His contributions to us: compassion, generosity, faithfulness, and love. It's not enough for us to honor God with our mouths, but He desires it from our hearts (Isaiah 29:13). When we delight ourselves in the Lord, seek Him first in everything we do, and make choices that reflect the place He has in our hearts, it is then when we bring the greatest honor to Him.

- **Cherish**—holding Him dear to your heart and knowing that nothing can separate you from His love (Romans 8:38–39).

- **Obey**—loving *how* He says to love (1 Corinthians 13:4–8) and hating *what* He says to hate (Proverbs 6:17–19). You must be willing to comply with His authority. Obedience to God—doing it His way instead of your way—shows Him that you love Him.

Love is like a disassembled gift that we receive but do not take the time to read the manual to assemble properly. You know how we open a package that has instructions and automatically just feel like we can do it without them? We'll toss those instructions aside and begin assembling the object, believing it is easy enough—only to find out in the end that the finished product does not work. We discover that we missed an important part or that we put parts together that were not designed to be used in that manner. In the end, it does not operate like the manufacturer designed it. God is the manufacturer, and we must walk out love by the manual—the Bible—to get the results that He has determined for us—good results. When we say that we are operating in love but find ourselves angrier than usual, more frustrated than usual, and less patient than before, this is an indication that we are not walking in love. If this is happening to you, then go back to 1 Corinthians 13. It specifies that love is patient and kind, and that it rejoices in truth and not in unrighteousness; love is not jealous, arrogant, or selfish, it does not hold grudges, and it is always hopeful and never gives up!

As Christians, we must operate in love. When we operate in love, we are operating in God because He is love. Operating in the spirit of love allows the gifts of the Holy Spirit (1 Corinthians 12:7–11) to be manifested in our lives with power. It also permits the fruit of the Spirit (Galatians 5:22–23) to come alive in us so we can be effective in this world. With love, our faith can work because faith works by love. Jesus commanded His disciples to love one another for by this men would know that they were His disciples. You are His disciple; you are a child of the Most High God … walk in love daily.

Not only is God's love unconditional, but it is also a choice. You can choose to accept it or reject it. God has given His only begotten Son, Jesus, for payment of our sins. Our Father made the choice to send His Son to the cross to die the death of a sinner, even though He sinned not, to make a way for us to come unto Him. As recipients, we now have everlasting life because He loved us. God knew that as Jesus was sown into the earth as a seed, through His death it would produce life … more sons (and daughters) in Jesus's name! Our Father knew that the benefit of His plan will outweigh the cost.

God wanted to bridge the gap that was made when Adam sinned. Man (human race) lost the connection with God, but thanks to God, the second Adam (Jesus) was sacrificed and reconciled us back to the Father. He endured pain and shame for us. He redeemed us from the curse of the law (2 Corinthians 3:6), and we now live under the blessings of God. Do you know that He knew you while you were being woven in your mother's womb? He had a plan for you since you were born. God is always reaching out to you. He'll never stop loving you—no matter what. He'll love you through the hurts and pains, past mistakes, and even present ones. His love is unconditional, so as you repent (turn away from that deed—not doing it again) He'll forgive you. The Bible says he'll cast it into the sea of forgetfulness as far as the east is from the west. Now that's far. You must remember, you are in a relationship with Him; therefore you, too, must forgive. Matthew 18:21–22 says, "Then Peter came and said to Him, "Lord, how often shall my brother sin against me and I forgive him? Up to seven times?" Jesus said to him, "I do not say to you, up to seven times, but up to seventy times seven." We must remember that God has forgiven us through Christ Jesus and so we must forgive others (Ephesians 4:32).

Forgiveness is a major part of the love walk with Christ. To love people is sometimes hard, but you now have the greater one (Holy Spirit) living in you, and He can assist you if you allow Him to. Remember, not your will (how you think or want to handle a situation), but God's will is to be done. You must forgive even though it hurts and even though they did *you* wrong. It

> *Forgiveness is a major part of the love walk with Christ.*

does not matter. You are not your own; you belong to God and must do it His way. Your obedience proves your love for Him. No need to fret; He'll be right there with you. He won't let you fall, and He won't let you down; therefore, give it all over to Him. He is on your side to give you the victory. Forgiveness is more for you than for the other person. If you do not forgive, you are carrying that person (the weight of the hurt) with you each and every day of your life ... and you wonder why you feel so exhausted and drained! Let that person go so you can be free—free to live, love, and laugh again. This is what God desires for your life. Forgiveness causes you to overcome the problem and go higher in Him.

Let me make something clear. When people say, "I'll forgive you, but I won't forget," they are not really forgiving you. They are choosing to hold on to the memory of the act, and it will always be with them concerning you. It will always be in their arsenal, so beware ... you will hear it again. I remember watching a sermon by a well-known pastor, and he mentioned that God's love is a game changer. When you do it His way, you'll never be the same again. As you forgive God's way, here's what happens. You will not forget the deed in the natural, but as you trust God with this care and the heaviness of it, you'll release it spiritually. One day when you see this person or the situation comes up in a conversation, you will not be affected by it like you used to. You will not have that anger rising up on the inside of you anymore. That stronghold will have lost its grip. You will be free! You will have peace and even compassion for them. This is how you know if you have truly forgiven in this situation. If you never reach this point, then you haven't forgiven. Remember, love does not keep a record of those who have wronged you, so let it go. You may say that it's too hard and I do not know what they did to you. You may feel like you can't let it go. I know it may be difficult, but if you do not forgive, then how can God forgive you? He won't. His word says, "*But if you do not forgive, neither will your Father who is in heaven forgive your trespasses*" (Mark 11:26). We live in this sinful world, and sooner or later you will need the Father to forgive you again. It is not worth you *not* being forgiven of God. Release it and experience His mercy.

You must always be conscious of His love—a compliment, a close parking space, or a discount when you weren't expecting it. You must learn that these are all acts of His love for you. Learn to be more thankful, for when you are, He'll do more. I truly believe it puts a smile on His face when we, His children, acknowledge His goodness and show appreciation for Him looking out for us.

Get a revelation of how much God loves you in your heart and hold on to it. Look up scriptures that speak of God's love for you. Then and only then can you operate in the unconditional love of God and bless others. You can't give away what you do not possess, so receive and embrace His love for you today. There is something else you must know about love, and that is love risks rejection. Rest in His unconditional love, and then you are free to love others without fear of rejection. Remember, loving God's way is not based on what someone else does or doesn't do for you. Rather it is based on your dedication to doing things God's way. Love is not forced; it comes willingly. As you sow this seed of love, guess what happens? It may be received or rejected. If rejected, that's okay. Do not get offended and go back to only loving conditionally … loving those who love you. Loving this way does not produce life, and you'll miss out on the joy that real love produces. But once received, it will create love in someone else's heart and they too can now be a recipient of God's love—receive Jesus Christ as Savior and Lord—and become a giver of it just like you! You can start a snowball effect with your love. Begin today to love courageously … you are an amazing, wonderful, and powerful creation of God. You are a product of His love!

Key #2

Trust

*Trust in the Lord with all your heart and lean not unto
your own understanding; in all your ways acknowledge
Him, and He shall direct your paths.* (Prov. 3:5–6)

Following and walking in God's word is going to require you to TRUST Him—Truly Rely Upon our Savior's Timing. It is all about timing with God. James 1:3–4 says it like this, "Knowing this, that the trying of your faith worketh patience. But let patience have her perfect work, that ye may be perfect and entire, wanting nothing." God is a strategic God, which means He has a specific plan for your life—one to give you an expected (good) end. You are not going to know everything up front and you are not going to get the whole picture at once, so what you have to do is have confidence in God that He is working behind the scenes for you! "For we walk by faith, not by sight" (2 Corinthians 5:7). You have to believe in what He says and not go on what you think. Just follow His leading. He loves you and wants to help you live this life effectively. He has given you everything that pertains to life and godliness (2 Peter 1:3). He's given you the Holy Spirit of promise to be with you on life's journey. Trust Him today.

In this world you will encounter trials and tribulations, but be of good cheer (confident, certain, take courage). Jesus, your Savior and Deliverer, has overcome the world. He has removed it of power to harm you and has defeated it for you (adapted from John 16:33 AMP).

Do you know what that means? Regardless of what you may go through, you are more than a conqueror through Jesus who conquered it all! You will get through the hurt, pain, misunderstanding, lack, or disappointment because Jesus has already conquered it for you. It's your job to stay in the fight and not give up because victory is on its way. Sometimes we must go through things that will cause us to pray and praise God more. This tends to draw us closer to Him and to know Him intimately in a way that we would have never known Him before. We will experience for ourselves how much He loves us, cares for us, and is faithful to what He has promised.

Understand this: as you go through your trial, God knows what you are going through. He allows the trial (it doesn't catch Him by surprise), He limits the trial (intensity, duration), and you will emerge victoriously once you learn from the test. As you go through your test, you may pray and not hear from God. Do not be alarmed and think that God has forgotten you. Not in the least. He is right there with you through it all, for He is Jehovah Shammah—the Lord is there. Remember, when we would take tests in school, the teacher was right there, but silent. The trial was designed to make you better, so do not become bitter in the process. Sickness and disease are not allowed by God to teach you a lesson; they come simply because we live in a fallen world and we are subject to the things that are here. Regardless, He wants us to go through trusting Him.

Let's take a look at Job. He was an upright man whom God referred Satan to because God knew Job was devoted and loved Him. Satan told God that if He would remove the hedge from around Job that he would curse God to His face. God knew otherwise and allowed Satan to test him but not to take his life. Job went through many difficulties and lost all he had: children and wealth.

In the end, Job emerged victoriously. Through the process, he had a deeper understanding of God and himself. He stated to God in Job 42:6, "Therefore I abhor myself, and repent in dust and ashes." You see, there was one thing that God needed to remove from Job and that was he was righteous in his own eyes and also justified himself rather than allowing God to justify him. Just as gold when it is being refined, the process causes the impurities to float to the top to be removed; so do our trials allow the impurities in our lives to become evident to us so that they, too, can be removed. These situations cause us to see ourselves and God more clearly. If we allow patience to have its perfect work in our lives, then we will be complete, wanting nothing. We will be in a better place with God. We will be operating like Him, talking like Him, and viewing life like Him. God has the best in mind for us. Romans 8:28 says that all things work together for the good of them that love the Lord. Go through it and learn the lesson needed for your spiritual growth. Oftentimes we stay in these tests longer than God may have originally designed because we're not "acting and receiving" correctly. Stop complaining and begin praising God, not for the test, but for your endurance, peace, patience, and ultimate victory over it.

There have been times when I had to trust God and back up from my thoughts and my feelings. It was not because I wanted to, but rather because I knew that if I wanted to get His results and to see Him show up and show out in the situation then I needed to get with His program. I had to act in a way that would please God and be patient. One time, my family was experiencing financial difficulty, and I thought I was trusting God in the situation. My mouth was saying all of the right scriptures and my heart believed or so I thought. My husband stated to me one day that my countenance was not of one who believed. I evaluated myself. You know, we are a three-part being—we are a spirit, we have a soul, and we live in a body. Well, my spirit was on board, but my soul (emotions) and body seemed to be lagging behind. The words were flowing from my lips, but my facial expression and my body movements were declaring otherwise. You know, it was like I wanted someone to ask, "What's wrong?" This would have been an opportunity to have a pity party by explaining my situation. No, this wasn't going to happen. So, I had to regroup and get back into reading scriptures that would help to elevate my beliefs in God's provision. In other words, I had to renew my mind (Romans 12:2) and get back my confidence in God. The joy of the Lord is our strength (Nehemiah 8:10).

You are going to have to do the same thing. Find scriptures on the subject you are standing and believing God for that will increase your faith and get your joy back! This will cause your spirit man to get stronger so you can make your soul and body get into agreement with God. Otherwise, you are not trusting in Him. You are wavering in your faith, and the Bible says in James 1:6–7, "But let him ask in faith, nothing wavering. For he that wavereth is like a wave of the sea driven with the wind and tossed. For let not that man think that he shall receive any thing of the Lord." Our Father cannot assist you when there is doubt. Doubt is sin. It diminishes your faith in His power because you are now letting what you think or believe supersede His word. In other words, you have made yourself god in the situation, and you will have to deliver yourself. That's not what He wants. He longs to be your deliverer, conqueror, defender, healer, and lawyer. He desires to be everything you need. He is not a man that He should lie or the son of man that He should repent (Numbers 23:19). He needs you to trust him totally, completely, and absolutely. It's not easy sometimes, but do it anyway. Our Father's way is tried and true. He'll make a way for you out of seemingly no way. Follow Him and you will get through. He is omniscient (knows everything), so trust Him.

In order to build a relationship with God and walk with Him daily, you have to get outside of your thinking. I know it is difficult to trust in someone you cannot see, but trusting means believing in what He says and just doing it. This is where your faith comes in. Now faith is the substance of things hoped for, the evidence of things not seen (Hebrews 11:1). Just because you can't see something doesn't mean it is not real. For example, the air you breathe, though you cannot see it, is real. When you speak, the words that come out of your mouth are real, the angels encamped around you right now are real, and Jesus is real too! Just because you cannot see them (Father, Son, and Holy Spirit) doesn't mean they are not real. It doesn't mean they cannot come to your rescue. Read the entire chapter of Isaiah 43 to see how God promises to rescue His people. You belong to Him; therefore, what is being said of the Israelites also refers to you. Get happy in your spirit. You are not alone in your situation. Jesus Himself, is fighting on your behalf. The spiritual world is more real than this physical world we live in. Everything you see came out of the spirit realm. So do not give up and do not give in because God will not give up on you … He is able. God loves you, and since you love Him, too, this is something you must do. Love is an action word, and trusting is an action … just do it!

Trusting God means to say only what the word says. Speak the word only! No matter how you feel, no matter how the situation looks … speak the word only. Do you remember your mom telling you, "If you do not have something nice to say, then do not say anything at all"? Well, the same goes with God. If your conditions are not the way you want them in your life, then do not say anything at all! Zip it.

What's been happening is this: we say what we see and continue to get what we say. We do not realize that we are putting a spiritual law into motion. God's word says that you shall have what you say (Mark 11:23). Speak the word of God over your situation so you can have it.

The world we live in was framed by God's words. He said let there be light, and light came into existence. Our words are creative. They are seeds, and they reproduce after their own kind. If you want to see something different then you must say something different. The old cliché says to keep doing things the same way, but expect a different result is insanity. You are not insane! Go and

> **We say what we see and continue to get what we say.**

begin reading the scriptures for what you need in order to build up your faith and begin to say that.

Do not put negative things out in the atmosphere. We've all said at one time or another, "bad things come in threes," "no one loves me," "I'll never be happy," "I'm holding up under the circumstances," or "I'm broke." Even speaking things in fun, if it is negative and contrary to God, then that, too, will come to fruition. An example would be, "I'm going crazy over here." Be careful because you may notice that you are beginning to experience trouble thinking clearly. Negative words have a tendency to go deep into your spirit. They tend to cause wounds that have lasting feelings of hurt, disappointment, anger, and even vengeance. The more you confess them, the more you are reinforcing them in your life. The only thing that has the power to undo, stop, and change the course of what has been set in motion is the word of God.

We must understand that our tongue is a small member of our bodies, but it can cause massive destruction. James 3:5 (NLT) says, "In the same way, the tongue is a small thing that makes grand speeches. But a tiny spark can set a great forest on fire." James wants us to know that our tongue is like kindling wood that is placed in a fireplace along with logs to start the fire. Once the fire is ablaze, you cannot find its source. When things are all out of control in our lives, it is hard to pinpoint where the trouble began. Most often than not, it began with our choice of words. If you do not want it, then do not say it. Say what you desire to have.

The enemy wants you to speak contrary to God's word. He wants you to believe that what you have been standing on is not coming to fruition because you may not see it yet. He does it in two ways; he increases your circumstances, and he causes you to recall every hardship. You begin to focus more on what's going on around you than your deliverer on the inside of you. This is how he pressures you into speaking what you see instead of what you want to see. The enemy knows that as you continue to speak contrary to God, those very words will ensnare you, causing you to be oppressed (downtrodden, depressed, and discouraged). He is a liar and the father of lies (John 8:44). The devil does not want you to be happy, prosperous, healthy, whole, or joyous, but God does. Say what God says so you can *have* what you say.

Trusting God means you are determined to wait upon Him until your change comes. Do not look to the left or the right, but stay your course. Stay focused on your mission (health, finances, marriage, employment, etc.). The Lord Jesus came so you may live this life more abundantly. It is His pleasure that you prosper and have every need of yours met so you can be a blessing to someone else (Genesis 12:2–3). You will be able to let someone know that patience is a virtue. You can tell them how you continued standing on the word of God and how He hastened to His word and performed it in your life. Share your testimony. It will be an encouragement to them. It will cause them to overcome the enemy that is trying to oppress them. The enemy is destroyed by the blood of the Lamb and the words of our testimony.

Key #3

Agree

Can two walk together except they be agreed? (Amos 3:3)

You cannot walk with God unless you come in agreement with His word. You must have the same opinion as God. You must will yourself to do, accept, and allow God's word (will) to be done and how He wills it to be done. Think about a couple in a relationship. If one wants to go left and the other right, unless they agree on which way to go, they will *not* be walking together. They will not be on the same page, and this will cause problems in the relationship. You may not understand why God will have you to do something in a particular way, but just do it anyway. Just trust His plan. He is working things out for you.

When we are in agreement with God, we have the same views and perspective as Him. We are harmonizing, responding, and resembling Jesus in the earth. Remember, people are watching. They hear what you say, but they also see what you do and if you are proclaiming to be a Christian, then your walk must match your talk. My bishop used to say, "The life we live speaks louder than the words we say." You see, the world says that talk is cheap, and it's true. We display our loyalty to Christ by our actions, not by wearing crosses around our necks, blasting gospel music from our cars, or quoting scriptures all day long. God is looking for true believers who keep their promise to serve Him all the days of their lives. James 1:22–25 says for us to be doers of the word and not hearers only. In other words, we must live our lives out loud and on purpose and then people will listen. We

> **"The life we live speaks louder than the words we say."**

21

must always remember that people in this world are hurting and are looking for the answer. We are the light that leads them to the answer … Jesus. If they cannot see the love, peace, and joy of the Lord in us, then it will be very difficult for them to experience the healing power of Jesus.

Christians have gotten a bad rap lately because we are not acting like Christians. We are not coming into agreement with God in every area of our lives. We allow situations and circumstances to determine how we act, instead of doing it God's way. We cannot have a bumper sticker on our car that says, "Jesus loves you" and when someone cuts us off we flip the bird. This is not a good representation of Christ. The world judges our genuineness not by who we confess to be, but by what they see us do, the choices we make, and the words we use. We must sound like and look like Jesus … every day. Here is the key: even if you miss it (do not do it like God said the first time), go back and make it right. This is still an opportunity for people to know that you serve God. If you say something you should not have said or the tone was wrong, apologize and ask for forgiveness. It, too, shows the love, consistency, and power of God in you. Our mission is for people to see Jesus in us every day.

If God's word says to pray for them that despitefully use you, then regardless of how you feel, you must pray and do good to them even though you know they have done you wrong. Do not work on getting even. Just leave that to God; His word says, "Vengeance is mine, I will repay." When you obey God and do it His way, guess what? You inherit a blessing (1 Peter 3:9). You see, the eyes of the Lord are on the righteous, and His ears are open to your prayers. He knows what you are going through and the difficulty thereof; but His face is against those who do evil.

Regardless of whether you are a child of God or not, if you fall into the "evil" category, there will be consequences you will have to face. So, do not do it … it's not worth it. You must remember this is a test. Go ahead, hold your peace, do what He says, and get the blessing! Please note: if or when you see the payback of God on those who have wronged you, do not rejoice in it. This displeases our Father because this act is evil in His eyes (Proverbs 24:17–18).

When you truly come into agreement with God, you will do things His way—no matter what. Coming into agreement with God helps to transform the way you look at things. You will begin to see things as

He sees them. Remember, it's not about you but about people seeing the power of God in you. With so much hatred, turmoil, and disbelief in the world nowadays, God is seeking no-matter-what Christians—no matter what comes or goes, no matter how it looks, and no matter how I feel, I'm going to do it God's way. Let it be you whom He finds operating like Jesus in the earth!

Key #4

Devote

*Commit your way to the Lord; trust also in him;
and he shall bring it to pass.* (Psalm 37:5)

In order to walk with God and build a relationship with Him, you must devote yourself to Him. In other words, give your life in totality to Jesus. Allow Him into every area of your life—home, church, work, children, marriage, business, etc.—so He can do whatever needs to be done to make your life great!

Romans 12 tell us how to dedicate our lives to God by making our bodies a living sacrifice unto Him. You must remember that you no longer belong to yourself but rather to God. The Lord Jesus paid the price for your life with His. He died the death of a sinner, even though He never sinned, so that you can live a life abundantly now and throughout eternity. You are *redeemed*!

As believers, we must show our gratitude by surrendering our fleshly desires to doing those things that please our Father. He has already made us righteous, and our job is to be holy and to live a set-apart lifestyle by no longer trying to blend in with the world. You must separate yourself from the way you used to behave, think, and speak and now submit yourself to doing things God's way. What does this mean, you might ask? You have to begin observing how you treat others (mistreat, ignore, belittle), how you talk to others (arguing, shouting, lying), and how you ponder situations (I can't do it, I'll never achieve it, it's too difficult). If those sound familiar then God wants you to replace those with patience, kindness, and hope. The more you do, the less you will feel the need to respond the "old" way. Devoting yourself to Him shows your love for Him.

You must also take what you do every day and do it as unto the Lord. Colossians 3:23-24 says, "And whatever you do, do it heartily, as to the Lord and not to men, knowing that from the Lord you will receive the reward of the inheritance; for you serve the Lord Christ." I took this scripture and literally applied it to my life and used it at work, in my marriage, with my children, and with anyone I dealt with. My supervisor asked me one day at work, "How do you get it all done?" I responded that I work as unto the Lord. You see, I do not work as unto my supervisor or manager, but I work to please my heavenly Father, and as I do that, things go well with me. And you know what? They will go well with you, too. Applying this scripture to your situations will cause you to be a better husband or wife, father or mother, student, employee, or business partner, not because you are trying to invoke benefits from the other person but because your heart is set on pleasing God. As you tackle circumstances in your life God's way, your life begins to exude praises to God!

There are three ways in a situation: the right way with wrong intentions, the wrong way, and God's way. Oftentimes we choose the wrong way because it's really what we want to do—save time, cut corners. We'll choose the right way, but we'll have wrong intentions because this way may cause us to look good and receive recognition. But choose God's way because it will be the right thing to do. You will be doing it for the right reason, and you will not be looking for a pat on the back—you'll have the right attitude in the matter. You see, when you do things just because it is the right thing to do, it makes you feel good on the inside. Everyone doesn't need to know everything you do. God sees, and He will reward you!

In the beginning of my walk with Christ, I used to struggle with this. I would think and I had even gone to God complaining about feeling like people were getting over on me because I was doing all of this work. He told me that no one could ever get over on me because He was with me. After that, I began to do what needed to be done regardless of whether I received assistance or if anyone noticed. To tell you the truth, it wasn't always easy to do. The enemy would bring things to my mind, show me people who could help, and try to use those tactics to make me angry. Oftentimes I had to press in hard to make sure I did not complain in the process. Complaining only stirs up negative emotions (anger, envy, strife), and the word of God says in James 3:16, "For where envying and strife is, there is confusion and every evil work." This is the devil's playground. This is exactly where he wants you to be, out of the will of God where he can kill, steal, and destroy you. The devil knows that God is not in the midst of confusion, so do not let him isolate you and back you into a corner. Stay with God.

While living this life with Christ, you will have to press through your emotions, attitudes, and desires. But one day, after being persistent in doing things the right way, you'll look up and realize that all this time you have been busily taking care of every area of your life God's way. You've learned the secret of devoting your life to Christ, and you are now receiving the reward of your labor—true peace! God's peace is strength, joy, and steadfast confidence in your faithful, all powerful, ever-present Father. His peace is His presence. When you are devoting yourself to Him, you are operating in the very presence of God. He's with you/ He'll never leave you or forsake you.

In a relationship in the physical, you want to please, honor, and dedicate yourself to the other person. It is even more so with the Father, who is committed to giving you and has already given you His best (Jesus Christ). You must focus on building your relationship with Him. True devotion will anchor your faith, enabling you to walk out God's word daily. Pray this prayer:

> Father, I surrender all; I give You my hands, my heart, my mind, my time, and my resources. I give them all to You today. I submit my will to You. I am Yours, so use me as You desire to accomplish Your will. Thank You for choosing me to partner with You today in Jesus's name.

Now, go on with your day expecting to see God step into your situation. Get ready to be used of Him. He's looking for willing vessels—those people who will say *yes* to His will and *yes* to His way. He loves those who are willing and obedient. The word of God says in Isaiah 1:19, "If ye be willing and obedient, ye shall eat the good of the land."

As you consecrate yourself unto the Lord daily, you show forth the love you have in your heart for Him. Devotion only works if it is coming out of a heart desiring to please God, not doing it out of obligation. Let your love for Jesus flow freely each day and see how God will abundantly bless you and more importantly, how He will make you a channel for blessing others in Jesus's mighty name!

> *Devotion only works if it is coming out of a heart desiring to please God, not doing it out of obligation.*

Key #5

Submit

Nevertheless not my will, but thine, be done. (Luke 22:42)

Submission to God means to come under His mission. Your assignment as a Christian is to live your life according to His plan. In the verse of scripture above, Jesus was about to die on the cross for you and me. It was a difficult moment for Him, yet He stated, "Not my will, but thine will be done." He knew God's plan was bigger than Him. He knew that God knew exactly what needed to be done and it would be great!

Submission is a choice, and in order to grow spiritually, you must choose to allow God to do His will in your life. Stop trying to fight or resist the word of God. Stop doing it your way, and do it God's way. Sometimes we need to get real with ourselves and ask this important question: "Has doing things my way caused me to be where I want to be in life?" If you are honest, the answer will be no. God has sanctified you and

> **Submission is a choice, and in order to grow spiritually, you must choose to allow God to do His will in your life.**

has separated you from the world's way of doing things. Those things that will cause you to fail. So, stop kicking against the pricks. You are only hurting yourself. Turn from your wicked ways—any thoughts or actions (cussing, lying, cheating, gambling, accusing, unforgiveness, worrying, doubting, gossiping, being unruly, etc.) that will cause you to sin. Respond to situations God's way, with love, patience, and self-control so that you can succeed.

You cannot straddle the fence and expect to walk out your

Christianity effectively. Your gifts, anointing, and the fruits you bear will be hindered because of it. There is a difference between the word and the world, and that difference is the L, which is the lie. The world has lied so much until even Christians have believed it. The world says and does things opposite of God. What God calls right, the world calls wrong; when God says no, the world says yes. God's way has benefits and brings

> *The law of creativity works on what you say, not on what you mean.*

success, while the world's way will only allow you to get so far before it pulls you down. There are so many clichés in the world that we have grown accustomed to. We do not even think about their meaning; we just say them. This is where we as Christians get into trouble. A few of them are: I'm scared to death, you are driving me crazy, and you take my breath away. These words all have negative meanings, and people will tell you that it's okay to say them because it's all in fun. What we are doing is allowing the enemy to say what he wants, and we are not refuting it. So what happens is this: these things begin to infiltrate your surroundings. You are a child of God who has the ability to create just as He does. What you say comes to pass—literally. The law of creativity works on what you say, not on what you mean. Therefore, say what you mean and mean what you say. It is very important that you understand how the words you speak can and will frame your life.

It's time to start curtailing the world's way by increasing God's way in your life. Walking with God will take some dedication on your part. What I have learned about being saved is to apply God's word to my life little by little. Do not focus on what you are doing wrong; just start doing things right … now. If you miss the mark, repent, get up, and do it again. "There is therefore now no condemnation to them which are in Christ Jesus" (Romans 8:1). Simply put—no guilt. Do not let the enemy try to keep you down with mistakes you have made in the past. You are forgiven. Do not believe the lie.

Now that you are saved, all those things you used to do will try to resurface and make you either feel ashamed or try to draw you back into them. Do not let them. You have been cleansed by the blood of Jesus. It takes away every stain (sin) and makes you white as snow. The Bible says it like this, "The LORD says, 'Now, let's settle the matter. You are stained red with sin, but I will wash you as clean as snow'" (Isaiah 1:18a GNT), and another scriptures says He casts them (sins) into the sea of forgetfulness. In other words, everything that was done before you received Christ, God doesn't remember them anymore. It is not that He doesn't remember them, because He is omniscient (knows all); but He chooses to forget and to wipe your slate clean, giving you a fresh start. He takes you back to your innocence as if you've never made a mistake, glory to God! He is not like man (humankind) who will say he has forgiven you, yet continue to remind you of your wrong. No, since He's said it, then that settles it, so go on with your life.

You may still suffer the consequences of those actions, but thank God He loves you so much that He doesn't pay you back in full for your wrongs. This is the grace factor kicking in. We no longer live under the curse of the law but under the blessings (grace) of God. Jesus paid the price for you and me, and because we have received Him, God's grace and mercy is upon us. The wages of sin is death, but the gift of God is eternal life through Jesus Christ our Lord (Romans 6:23).

What He has done is separated you from your sins as far as the sunrise is from the sunset (east and west). You see, God's love for you is so great that He used the largest distance to describe where He's thrown your sins. Picture the earth. If you begin traveling south from the North Pole, eventually you will begin heading north again once you reach the South Pole. That can be measured. While east and west are infinite, the earth is a sphere; therefore, if you begin walking east you will continue east forever without end. What's so great about it is the sin is no longer yours. Jesus paid the price for you to go free, for whom the Son sets free is free indeed. Now this is what He says concerning you, so believe it, and when the enemy comes in to bring a lie, just remind him of what the God of the universe has said about you. Jesus has forgiven you; it's time for you to forgive yourself and to move forward with your new life.

In the physical, people may look at being submissive in a negative way. It can be when you are submitting yourself to someone or something that is taking advantage of you, but not with God. He only has your best interest at heart. In the physical, submission may look like you are being weak. On the contrary, submission to God shows your confidence in

31

Him to provide, strengthen, love, change, and guide you, ensuring that you will fulfill the plan, purpose, and destiny that He has set for your life.

Submission means to prefer someone over yourself. It's an act of selflessness instead of selfishness. That's strength! When you prefer someone, this usually leads to them preferring you. You cannot lose when you are following God's way of doing things. When Jesus asked God, His Father, "Is there another way to do this?" (salvation), He quickly stated, "Not my will, but thine will be done." He went through it so that God could be glorified. In the end, God glorified Jesus and set Him at His right hand in a position of authority, where He is seated today. In 1 Peter 5:6 the word of God says, "Humble yourselves therefore under the mighty hand of God, that he may exalt you in due time." Be patient. God will promote you at the right time. He's lining things up so when the day of elevation arrives, you will be all that He has called you to be. People will see all that you have accomplished and give praise to you, and you will turn around and say, "I could not have done it had it not been for the Lord." This brings glory to God, and He in turns blesses you. It's a win/win situation. You cannot fail with the God who prevails!

We all subject ourselves to one another in servanthood. Parents tenderly give themselves to their children; doctors caringly give themselves to their patients; and Jesus lovingly gave Himself for us … this is submission God's way. In the world, people fight for their rights, not to be subjected under someone else, but God's way causes us to serve each other in love. Therefore, each of us is benefited in the end. Jesus

> *Great and rewarding recognition does not stem from your title but from you living your life pleasing before God.*

had authority over His disciples, yet He submitted himself to them and washed their feet. Great and rewarding recognition does not stem from your outward position or title but from your inward stance toward living your life in a pleasing way before God.

Key #6

Humble

*Humble yourselves in the sight of the Lord,
and he shall lift you up.* (James 4:10)

Humility shows that you are connected to God. Jesus did not come to be served, but to serve. Jesus humbled Himself even unto the death of the cross, and God gave Him a seat at His right hand in a position of authority. Recognize that being a servant is the key to promotion and receiving honor from God.

Humility is a fruit of the Spirit, and it is one that is quite illusive. Those that think they have it do not, and those that do not actually do. Humility enables you to have a teachable spirit. Being humble means there is no need to defend yourself, causing arguments. You have the power to defuse arguments because a soft answer turns away wrath. You can also talk with the right attitude by not allowing unwholesome words to proceed out of your mouth, but only that which is good to edify those listening.

It's all about understanding that the God who created the universe created you, and your very breath depends on Him, while also understanding that no man is an island and you cannot do everything by yourself ... you need people. When you embrace these truths, you begin to appreciate God for who He is and those whom He has placed in your life.

Here is how you can begin to operate in humility:

- *Take responsibility for your actions—no more excuses.*
- *Allow God's word to be first place and final authority in your life— respond God's way, not your way.*
- *Be compassionate.*

- *Put others first.*
- *Give others the benefit of the doubt; do not be so quick to judge a situation.*
- *Do not think higher of yourself than you ought to neither allow the enemy to cause you to think lower of yourself (low self-esteem)— balance is the key; believe what God has said about you.*

Psalm 100:3 says, "It is He that hath made us and not we ourselves. We are His people and the sheep of His pasture." This is the natural order of things. God should always be at the forefront of our actions and thoughts. When we are prideful, it's just like we figure we have orchestrated our lives and almighty God is just an afterthought. At this point, we tend to make ourselves the creator and not the creation. Luke 6:40 (AMP) says, "A pupil is not superior to his teacher, but everyone [when he is] completely trained (readjusted, restored, set to rights, and perfected) will be like his teacher." Our Father wants us to be like Him. He wants us to act like Him and demonstrate His power in the earth.

When we give ourselves the credit for all things going right or well, we then make ourselves god over it. It's an ego thing! Isn't it funny how people tend to take the credit when all is going well, yet blame God when things go wrong? Personally, I do not think it is fair to Him. If you're going to blame Him when things are bad, then why not credit Him when things are good … right! No one wants to take responsibility for their actions, but they swiftly take the recognition when conditions are favorable. This is truly the world's way of doing things.

In today's times, people often say, "Where was God?" when tragedy hits. He is always with us. Unfortunately, we have taken Him out of schools; therefore, His protection is out, and drugs, gangs, and violence are in. We have backed away from His principles, and we now see laws being passed that are not of God. Yet, people want Him to swoop in and save the day against terrorism and other acts of violence. They do not understand that when we operate outside of His will (the Bible), we then separate ourselves from His divine peace, protection, and provision. Many do not want to believe it, but it is true. Men have become lovers of themselves. Second Timothy 3:2–4 says it like this, "For men shall be lovers of their own selves, covetous, boasters, proud, blasphemers, disobedient to parents, unthankful, unholy, without natural affection, trucebreakers, false accusers, incontinent, fierce, despisers of those that are good, traitors, heady, high-minded, lovers of pleasures more than lovers of God." This is what we are experiencing today, and it is totally opposite of God's desires for us. Yet, because He is a good God, they figure He is supposed to just step in and render aid without people even acknowledging their wrong. It's always a heart matter with God. He gives us chance after chance. How many times will God continue to grant forgiveness to stubborn-hearted individuals who only want what they want and only call Him when things are out of control?

It's all about understanding that we have been given a free will—a will to make our own decisions. God desires us to love and honor Him because we want to, not because He makes us. Think about a parent who loves his child. It's a special moment when his child comes and says, "I love you," not because the child feels pressured but because it is coming from a pure and sincere heart. It is the same with God.

We should never get caught up in self-praise. It doesn't look good on us. A child of God doesn't wear that cloak well. In actuality, this is not God's plan for our lives. He wants us, His children, to acknowledge Him in all things and praise Him in the good times and in the not-so-good times. We do not praise Him for the situation but for being with us through the situation, knowing that He will never leave us or forsake us. He's always right there. By acknowledging God in your successes (knowing that you could not have achieved it without Him), you are now walking in true humility. Even when your circumstances are not good, press in to praise. It may be difficult at first, but in a moment, the joy of the Lord will begin to arise in your heart and you will begin to remember His faithfulness to you in times past.

> *By acknowledging God in your successes, you are now walking in true humility.*

We must understand that God is Elohim, the creator God. Looking back to Genesis 1, you will see how the earth was without form and it was void. The only ones on the scene were God, Jesus, and the Holy Spirit. God then began to say, "Let there be ..." and then what He had spoken came into existence. After that, our Father saw that it was good.

You see, all God does is good. We cannot explain why things happen the way they do sometimes, but we must remember that He's with us through it, He has a plan, and His plan is always good.

We now see that adoration and praise should only go to God. Otherwise, if given to ourselves, it becomes pride (arrogance, pretentious, vain). Here is why God abhors pride. Being prideful is like a balloon that is so full of air that eventually it will pop! An example of this will be a balloon being visualized as humankind, a string attached to the balloon is humility and the helium in the balloon is pride. Pride is not a bad thing in some instances because as we have humility along with it, God has us. If we are disconnected from humility, then humankind is separated from God and flies high and eventually comes to destruction. In the book of Proverbs 16:18 (MSG) the word of God says, "First pride, then the crash—the bigger the ego, the harder the fall."

Take a look at King Nebuchadnezzar in Daniel 4. He allowed himself to be consumed with pride; therefore, he fell. He had a dream that deeply disturbed him and Daniel interpreted it for him. God gave him a year to repent, and he did not. One day, Nebuchadnezzar was proclaiming his greatness in how he built the kingdom for his majesty, but before he could utter anything else, a voice from heaven said, "O king Nebuchadnezzar, to thee it is spoken; the kingdom is departed from thee" (Daniel 4:31). Nebuchadnezzar was driven from men, ate grass like animals, his hair grew and was matted, and his nails were like birds' claws. He remained in this state for seven years. When pride comes in, your judgements are blurry and your mind is unclear. When you recognize God's authority, positioning, and greatness, your mind then becomes clear again. Nebuchadnezzar summed it all up like this in verses 34 and 37 in the Message Bible:

> At the end of the seven years, I Nebuchadnezzar, looked to heaven. I was given my mind back and I blessed the High God, thanking and glorifying God, who lives forever. ... I Nebuchadnezzar singing and praising the King of Heaven; Everything He does is right and He does it the right way. He knows how to turn a proud person into a humble man or woman.

God is smart. He already knows the outcome of a prideful life. He doesn't desire this for you. You are an amazing creation. By receiving Jesus as Savior and Lord of your life, you are royalty. You are now a king and priest of the Most High God! You are an heir of God and a joint heir with Jesus, which means that what Jesus has, you have! You are already significant. You do not have to promote yourself; let God do it. You are to humble yourself so that God in due time will exalt you. But if you reverse the plan of God and exalt yourself, then God Almighty has no other choice but to humble you. This is not a pretty sight. This is not the plan God has for you.

You are on an assignment from God to exhibit His trait of humility in the earth. Humility is simply having a servant's heart. I was always told that a good leader must first be a good follower. In order to lead your family, supervise coworkers, or head up a neighborhood committee, you must first learn to humble yourself to those in authority. Life is like a boomerang; whatever you put out is what's coming back to you. You cannot expect to have everyone following your directions if you are not first willing to submit to others. Do not be like Nebuchadnezzar and miss your blessing because of a prideful heart. Allow your life and your love for God to demonstrate His character in you. Give Him permission to use you, His servant, today so He can do what He truly desires, which is to promote you!

Key #7

Ask Every Day

Therefore I say unto you, what things soever ye desire, when ye pray,
believe that ye receive them, and ye shall have them. (Mark 11:24)

Ask the Holy Spirit every day for guidance. This is the part I love to do. Since I know that I can do nothing without the Lord, I ask Him every day for favor, insight, open doors, and opportunities. I welcome the Lord into each day and thank Him for what He's done, doing, and about to do in my life. I even write letters to the Father about anything and everything. This is the time where you can truly fellowship with the Lord Jesus Christ how you desire. You can talk with Him or you can sing to Him on the way to work or school, or even in the shower. Regardless of how you do it, just do it. I promise you it will jump start your day!

The word of God says, "Ask and you shall receive, seek and you shall find, knock and the door shall be opened to you" (Matt.7:7). Just ask the Father and believe that you have already received and go about you day in peace. Do not be afraid to ask the Lord for what you need every day … He loves it when you do. Communication is the key to any good relationship. It shows that He is your source.

There are many scriptures in the Bible that speak on asking. It is all summed up to your belief. When you approach God with a request, you must believe that you receive when you pray. You know, God is just like our natural parents who love to answer the requests of their children. But even we as parents evaluate a situation to see if the child is ready for the gift. Even more so for our heavenly Father. He is so wise that He knows what we need, what we desire, and what is good for us. He will not give us something that will hurt us. If you cannot handle $100 then why would God give you $1,000? You will waste it and still be in the same position or worse. That's not what God desires for your life.

God is Jehovah Jireh, our provider. He knows our needs and provides for them. When we approach God, we must ask according to His will, and we must know that He hears us. If we ask anything outside of His will, we are asking amiss. We also cannot be double-minded (doing a little God's way and a little the world's way) and expect to receive from Him.

Whenever you ask God for something, continue to give Him praise thereafter. If the answer doesn't come right away, just keep standing in faith. If you discover that you have gotten angry with God because He didn't respond instantaneously, then take a look at yourself. Were you believing when you prayed? Probably not. Remember, everything with our Father is a heart issue. He looks at the heart of the matter—are we in faith or do we have an ulterior motive. These are some of the things He is looking for. He wants us to trust Him and be sincere when we pray. Another reason for unanswered prayer is that whatever we are praying for may not be God's best, and as we just continue to trust (rely on His timing), we'll see the rewards of patience ... it'll be exceedingly, abundantly, above all that we could ask or think!

I remember when my husband was looking for a car. We went to one dealership that was close to home and were pretty much scolded by the salesman. The sad part in this situation was the salesman was training a new employee. We were disappointed with the way we were treated so we left and noticed the trainee also looked hurt in the process. My husband and I said that this was not our car and continued to believe for God's best. Then we found the same type of car listed for a better price, the right color, and more options, but it was two hundred miles away. My husband contacted the sales agent, and we took a drive. The first thing we noticed when we arrived at the car lot was a difference in the atmosphere; it was peaceful, pleasant, and caring. The sales rep was so kind, informative, and patient. We then went to the financial officer, and his demeanor was the same. We drove home with a new car and a great experience. This was "our" car, and it was God's best for us!

What to do after you pray: begin to praise and offer thanksgiving for the answered prayer even if the situation has not changed. Your stance must always be "it's already done" regardless of what you see. The world says seeing is believing, but it's not true because once you see it, there's no need to believe or hope for it. The Christian's mantra is, "I believe; therefore I see." In your heart you must know that it is a done deal. Stand still and see the salvation (rescue) of the Lord. It's coming ... oh, yes it is! Some things are done instantaneously and others are achieved through a process. Whichever method God deems appropriate, just be willing to wait. Patience is a virtue. Patience is a fruit of the Spirit. It's all coming together for your good. God is a strategic God, and He knows the precise moment to bring things to fulfillment. What God has for you ... it's for you!

Key #8

Meditation and Application

This book of the law shall not depart out of thy mouth; but thou shalt meditate therein day and night, ... for then thou shalt make thy way prosperous, and then thou shalt have good success. (Joshua 1:8)

What you think about is very important on your journey with Christ. If you are not careful, consider this from Frank Outlaw:

Watch your thoughts; they become words
Watch your words; they become actions
Watch your actions; they become habits
Watch your habits; they become your character
Watch your character; it becomes your destiny. (O'Toole, 2013)

Thoughts are unspoken words, and words are seeds; therefore, you must sow wisely. An apple seed when planted will one day grow into a large tree and contain many apples. The same is true with the words that you speak. One day they, too, will mature and reproduce after their kind shaping your destiny, whether good or bad. Sowing God's word will produce good fruit in your life, while sowing words contrary to God will result in you receiving bad (negative) outcomes. I implore you to speak words that will bring forth life and prosperity for you and your posterity.

It all starts by meditating on the word of God daily. It will allow you to retain and better understand it. Ask the Holy Spirit to bring clarity to your understanding of God's word. Just knowing scriptures and being able to recite them is not enough. Satan knows the scriptures, and he will distort them to get you to disobey God. He tried it with Jesus in

Matthew 4:1–11, but Jesus also responded with the word: "It is written …" You must hide the word of God in your heart and hold fast to it. This is your lifeline. The enemy of your faith comes to kill, steal, and destroy you, but God's word is a shield to those who take refuge in Him. You must apply God's word to everything you do. You must do what it says to do, act how it says to act, say what it says to say, and

> *Satan knows the scriptures, and he will distort them to get you to disobey God.*

live how it says for you to live. Your very life depends upon it. God told Joshua that as he meditates on the word he would have good success. You will be victorious in every area of your life as you get His word in you. When tested, you will be squeezed, and what will come out of you will be what is *most* in you. If there's more world, then you will react according to your old man (fighting, swearing, doubting, screaming, antagonizing, etc.). If it's more word, then you'll respond with peace, patience, and positive actions. Out of the abundance of your heart your mouth will speak. Make sure when the pressure comes it's His word and His principles that are displayed so you can obtain His victory—glory to God!

People usually want to know how to apply God's word to their lives. I say to merely follow suit. An example would be Colossians 3:23, "And whatsoever ye do, do it heartily, as to the Lord and not unto men." In any area of your life (marriage, home, work, school, friends), do things that will please God. While at work, work as unto the Lord, not your supervisors. In other words, regardless if your supervisor is there or not, continue doing your very best. Do not do it for a pat on the back but just knowing that God Almighty is watching. Do it because you want to please Him. Trust me, He will be pleased! He loves it when His children operate in His character. Just like in the natural a father is pleased when his children follow after him, so with our heavenly Father. We are to be imitators of Him. When you do, you are bringing glory to God and representing Him *well*!

Another example of walking out His word is to make sure you are not just declaring it but applying it. I was declaring the scripture Psalm 75:6 that promotion doesn't come from the east, west, or south, but promotion is of the Lord. One day I was convicted by the Holy Spirit. At that very moment, I was reminded of Hebrews 4:13, which says that nothing is hidden from God's sight. Everything we do is exposed, and we must give an account for it. All of a sudden, I began to recollect the times I was tardy. I became overwhelmed by my slothfulness as it flooded my remembrance. Wow. That hit me right in the gut. You see, I used to drag into work, just getting in under the wire. I had to be at work by 8:30 a.m., and I would arrive sometimes at 8:29, 8:31, or even 8:35 a.m., just making it in that "grace" period. God gives us grace (unmerited favor) every day, but we should not abuse it.

Sometimes people think because we live under grace (freedom from sin) it gives us an out to commit sin and just repent. Not so. Grace is there for us, believers, to remember God's love and forgiveness. Let's take a quick look at what grace is. Grace is God's redemptive power for all people. In other words, it's His favor being poured on sinners who do not deserve it. He does not desire men to perish, but that they will come to repentance. Grace also gives Christians the power to say no to sin. Humanity inherited the sin nature once Adam and Eve disobeyed God's instructions. This means that even if you're doing everything seemingly right and not lying, stealing, or cheating, you still cannot enter heaven because the sin nature hasn't been dealt with. This nature cannot come into the presence of God. You must be born again (receive salvation through Jesus, which is the new birth) in order to remove this covering from your life. Once you are born again, temptations will come, but you do not have to submit to them. Grace gives you the strength to choose God's way in the matter.

Now going back to my situation, in my case, I was taking advantage of the seven minutes given by my employer. Our employers do not have to give us a grace period, but thank God most of them do. Why? It helps us when life happens. You see, I was not considered late by the organization, but this was not good enough for God. God doesn't want slackers. He needs someone who is diligent, consistent, energetic, and lively. Otherwise, do not expect Him to show up and show out in your situation because He won't. God will not bless a mess. He cannot stand by that ... it's not His word. He only hastens to His word to perform it.

If I wanted Him to promote me, guess what? He wasn't, not with my track record. Promotion and anything else from God can only come by us operating by His principles and precepts. So please when you are applying God's word to your situation and believing Him for something, make sure you are doing exactly what you are supposed to do. There is to be no slacking, no dragging, no slothfulness, only faithfulness. As for me, I got my act together and after a while, I began to see our Lord do some great things in my life. He began to open doors for me and gave me favor. He continues to favor me, and I am so grateful to Him for it. I tell you the truth, it works. If He did it for me, He'll do the same for you. You see, God is not a respecter of persons (Romans 2:11), but He is a respecter of faith. Now this is His word, and He will hasten to it to perform it!

Also, when you are walking out God's word in your day-to-day living, be sure that you are not doing it for selfish reasons because God knows your heart. Man looks at the outer appearance, but God sees the heart. He knows if you are sincere or not. So, do what is right, because it is right, and then do it right. Do it with the right heart, the right attitude, and the right motive. I cannot say it enough, everything with God is a heart matter. Therefore, your motive is crucial when desiring to please God.

When you begin applying the word of God to your life, do not fear making mistakes. God did not give you a spirit of fear, but of power, love, and a sound mind. We all miss it from time to time, but just make sure that your ultimate goal is to please God. As you do, God knows it, and the Holy Spirit will step in to assist you. He is your guide, comforter, teacher, and revealer.

> *Your destiny is in your mouth.*

The Holy Spirit will divulge to you what and how to accomplish your objective. He did it for me when I was declaring promotion, and He will surely do it for you, too. Just as He instructed me to get up early in order to arrive early, He'll show you how to maneuver yourself to receive from God. I'm going to let you in on a little secret: God wants to bless you more than you can even imagine! All He's looking for is someone willing to do it His way. Your destiny is in your mouth. Continue meditating and speaking the word of God daily and applying it to your situations so you can have the victory in them all. You are His success story!

Key #9

Walk by the Spirit

*Walk by the Spirit and ye shall not fulfill the
lust of the flesh.* (Galatians 5:16)

Now that you are saved, committed to God and His principles, you have to live the way citizens in your new kingdom live. It is now time to begin letting go of the way you used to behave and handle situations before you got saved. The first thing you need to know about walking in the Spirit is there are no more crutches. You do not have to depend on the schemes you used to do and say to get you out of trouble. Instead, rely on the gifts of the Spirit and the word of God.

No more excuses—we can get hung up on the fact that we are humans and use this as a crutch when we get in trouble. It is so easy to begin using those things we used to do back in the world system before we got saved. Remember, we would say, "I did this because, you know, I am only human." That's another lie from the pit (enemy). You are not *only* human, but rather a spirit that has a soul and lives in a body. You are a child of the Most High God, who has His Spirit living in you. The Holy Spirit in you is greater than the spirit that is in the world that's trying to get you to back away from your new life. But he is a liar.

In and of yourself you are weak, bitter, spiteful, boastful, and manipulative. But you do not have to settle for this. You have a higher standard to strive for. You have God on your side. When situations want to cause you to respond in your humanity, remember that God is strong, merciful, kind, humble, and gracious. Lean on Him and His qualities. It's hard sometimes, but you have to press into the things of God and deny what and how the flesh wants you to feel. Cut off the provisions for the flesh and do not give the flesh what it needs in order to do what it wants. It wants you to act ungodly, so instead of arguing, just give a soft answer because a soft answer turns away wrath. You have to say, "I will not act, speak, or think anything other than the word of God." It's time to take control of your life.

Hold your peace—God will fight your battles. You must stay at peace with people. Remaining in control only happens when you are disciplined. Being in control is a lifestyle, and it is directed toward pleasing God. Hold your peace and God will show up on your behalf.

Keep your joy—the joy of the Lord is your strength. It is a fruit of the Spirit that dwells in you. It is a powerful force used to defeat discouragement. The world didn't give it to you, and the world cannot take it away. Keep your joy and you'll keep the power.

Be thankful—let God know that you are thankful for what He has done in your life. First Chronicles 16:8 says, "Give thanks unto the LORD, call upon his name, make known his deeds among the people." Live to find the good in your life. Do not be a complainer; be a praiser! In the process, let others know of what He's done for you. Who knows? Your testimony could be the very thing that God uses to draw them to Christ.

Expect great things—having expectancy is the key to walking in the Spirit. It shows your confidence in your God. Expect God to show up and show out in your life in every situation and circumstance. He perfects those things that concern you (He fulfills His purpose in your life). He has good thoughts on His mind for you—thoughts to give you a future and a hope.

I've heard Pastor Mingo say, "When you walk in the Spirit you always win because you are never dominated by your emotions or external factors." You are operating in the fruits of the Spirit, which are love, joy, peace, patience, kindness, goodness, faithfulness, and self-control. Walking in the Spirit keeps you from fulfilling the lusts of the flesh. The lusts of the flesh are factors that stimulate your senses, and they will cause you to walk in error. The devil wants to trip you up, but God has a plan for you to withstand all temptations. You triumph over his tactics by continuously walking in the Spirit.

> **When you walk in the Spirit you always win because you are never dominated by your emotions or external factors.**
> **-Pastor H. Mingo**

Key #10

Be Persistent

Even so faith, if it hath not works, is dead, being alone. (James 2:17)

In the world, there is a cliché that says practice makes perfect, which means the more you do something the better you will get at it. Practice is training, rehearsal, and preparation. It's a little different in God's system. With God, you need to be persistent—tenacious, resolute, continuous, tireless, and patient. God thinks deeper than we can imagine. To me, practicing just scratches the surface of living, while being persistent goes to the core of your very being. It is more like you have a goal and you are determined to reach it, no matter what. You are remaining on course regardless of opposition or difficulty. God wants you to develop strength and character to be the person He has called you to be. Persistency is the vehicle that will get you there.

In order to be able to see the benefits of God's word and see your life change, you must continue to work the word—you must be consistent. You may make mistakes; you may not see any results at first, but keep on doing things God's way. This builds character. You will not master this overnight, but in your steadiness, you will master it.

You must operate in self-control. The enemy comes to kill, steal, and destroy, so keep your focus. Remember, this life is not about you but all about Christ who lives in you. The fight that we face is really not about us either. The enemy is angry with Jesus, so he attacks you and me (His inheritance). "Be not afraid nor dismayed … ; for the battle is not yours, but God's" (2 Chronicles 20:15). Do not let your emotions and feelings hold you captive. The fight is not necessarily with the person in front of you rather the spirit behind the person. Please note: anyone can be used at any time by the devil—even Christians. Yes, you and I, if we are not careful, can become argumentative and start confusion. We do not wrestle with flesh and blood but rather spirits in high places. When situations come against you, you must press through and see in the spirit what's really going on. The enemy wants you to be in strife because where there is chaos, every evil work is present. When you are a participant in discord, you have now removed yourself from God's covered protection. You need the God of deliverance to be with you always. So do not be duped by the devil. You can stand. You can hold your peace and operate in the power of God.

His word says in James 4:7, "Submit yourselves therefore unto God. Resist the devil and he will flee from you." When situations come against you, hold fast to God's character in you. Do not respond to the act with the world's remedy ... handle it God's way. As you submit to God and His word, you begin building up your resistance to the devil's temptations (turning your back to his enticements) and he loses any foothold against you. This is how you resist the devil and he will flee from you. Your weapons are not carnal (fleshy) but mighty to the pulling down of strongholds. Did you know that your peace is a weapon, your joy is a weapon, and your testimony of what God has done for you is a weapon in your arsenal? You are something going somewhere to happen! The world will take notice of the godliness and fortitude in you.

You must be diligent in serving the Lord and building a relationship with Him. Now is not the time to give up, throw in the towel, or even drag your feet. You are on a mission for God! Diligence shows others that you are all about business ... God's business. You are a go-getter for Christ.

The more you commit yourself to doing what's right, the easier it will get, and before you know it, you have developed a lifestyle of living righteous, holy, honorable, and pleasing before God. See, I told you, you can do it!

Just Doing Church

Being saved is more than just going to church. If you are not careful, you can get caught up in tradition or better put "religion." This is putting more effort and priority on how to serve God (going to church every Sunday) rather than keeping your focus on how God wants to be served (pleasing God every day). It can actually cause you to be bound. Being religious is very dangerous. It will cause one to be a hypocrite to the faith. In Luke 13:14 the synagogue leaders were upset with Jesus for healing a woman on the Sabbath. They claimed, "There are six days for work. So come and be healed on those days, not on the Sabbath." Religion would rather argue about dates instead of seeing someone delivered. You can easily get caught up in self efforts and works, and the results will leave you feeling guilty or extremely angry. God's way is for His people to experience liberty, for 2 Corinthians 3:17 says, "Where the Spirit of the Lord is there is liberty." There is freedom in worshiping the Lord. In the process, He will give you peace, joy, and power in order to deliver, heal, and set the captives free. It is all about continuously operating in the love of God.

Church is an excellent place to be because this is where you get your training (gain leadership skills). At my church, our motto is "training people to the glory of God." It is also your filling station. You come to get filled up and go back into the world to release it all by sharing what you've learned and putting God's truths into operation. At church, you get fed the word of God, work out your salvation by joining a ministry to serve others, fellowship with your brothers and sisters in Christ, learn to reorder your priorities, and get encouragement. You also come to worship the Lord in giving through the paying of your tithes (10 percent of income due to God) and giving offerings unto Him. It's not about you just "doing" church but rather building your relationship with Him. It all starts by doing the above mentioned with a heart that desires to please God.

Going to church should not be viewed as a burden but rather a pleasure. We should be excited when it's time to go to church. David said in the book of Psalms, "I was glad when they said unto me, let us go into the house of the Lord" (Psalm 122:1). Oftentimes we think that we've done our duty for the day after attending service. I know because at one point in my life, I felt the exact same way. I believed, "Since I've gone this morning I'm free to do what I want the rest of the day." I was looking at it in the wrong manner. I wasn't building a relationship with God the way He wanted it. No, I was fulfilling what I thought was satisfactory as a Christian. Having this opinion will lead you to become a carnal Christian—immature in faith and having behavior motivated by fleshy desires. In other words, you will begin to do more of what *you* want to do and less of what God wants you to do. Beware, carnality is a very dangerous state to be in. It will cause you to believe that you are exercising your faith and walking close with God because you are doing somethings according to the word, like going to church, reading your Bible at times, or saying hallelujah, only to find out later that you have been moving farther and farther from Him. Sometimes you may not realize this until it's almost too late. You can avoid this by staying in God's word and obeying all of it, not picking and choosing what parts you like, and simply asking God to show you yourself. He will and it may not be pretty, but it will reveal where you are in your love walk so you can begin to make the necessary changes to get back on track with Him.

Just going to church to say I've been to church is the wrong attitude for attending. If someone asks, "How was church today?" and you respond, "It was just church," that displays your type of relationship with God. If you didn't put anything into it, then quite naturally, you won't get anything out of it. You have to go anticipating and expecting to meet with God, to learn something new, or to receive an answer to your prayer. Without expectation and personal input you will not receive anything from the Lord.

Enter into God's house single-mindedly. Do not get caught up in what may be happening around you. If the usher asks you to move to another location, if the greeter is not pleasant, or if someone steps on your toe, just keep your peace. Please do not react cruelly, but rather respond with kindness. Proverbs 3:3 (NASB) says, "Do not let kindness and truth leave you; Bind them around your neck, Write them on the tablet of your heart." You must stay focused on your purpose for coming, and that is to commune with the almighty God who is your Father. You cannot allow anything to separate you from this moment. It's your deliverance, healing, or the answer to your prayer that's on the line. Situations of this sort are designed by the enemy to cause you to miss out on your blessing. He wants you to be so aggravated that you will focus more on the situation and less on the service. The devil is a liar, you will receive what your Father God has for you. You will obtain the victory and receive your breakthrough. Do not be deceived. A double-minded man is unstable in all his ways and *will not* receive anything from the Lord; yet, a single-minded man is stable in all his ways and *will* receive of the Lord. Stay focused.

I once heard a pastor say that we come to church to be informed of God, but we get to know Him through our personal study time. Whatever you do, do not neglect your personal time with the Lord. It helps you to be transformed into the image of Christ. You gain a deeper, more intimate relationship with Him, and you'll begin to see the world from His perspective.

Going to church makes you feel wonderful, but the purpose is to come and meet with God. Most churches have praise and worship before the service begins. This is your time to get in the presence of God, to help set the atmosphere for miracles to take place, and to allow the Holy Spirit free reign so that He can draw others to Jesus. This also prepares the way for the word of God to flow with ease from the pastor or minister and be received by the congregation.

One thing that people have a tendency to do is to unknowingly put their *faith* and *confidence* in the pastor, and sadly if he falls then they, too, fall. Their spirits are crushed, and they feel as though there is no use in serving God. They tend to back up from the things of God and leave church altogether. This is not the plan of God. If you ever experience something of the sort, remember that God loves you and longs for you to remain in the fold. The word of God says not to forsake the assembly of the saints, in other words, it's imperative to your faith that you gather and communicate with your brothers and sisters in Christ. We get strength and encouragement through these relationships, and the Bible calls it iron sharpening iron. When we gather together, the anointing flows from one to another, but you must be a participant. God's desire is for us to follow our pastor as he or she follows Christ. Our faith and focus is on the Lord Jesus Christ, the One who saved us.

People make choices in life, some of which may be detrimental, but do not let this discourage you in your walk with Christ. He is perfect, and He uses imperfect men to perfect others. If that person should fall, let not your heart be troubled. Pray and seek God's face and His will for your life. He may tell you it's time to leave and He will direct you to another church, but then again, He may tell you to stay because that house (church) is teaching His word effectively. The pastor or minister will be reprimanded by the church, and he also has to deal with God. Prayerfully, he will repent and return to God. Luke 6:37 says, "Judge not, and ye shall not be judged." You are not to gossip, criticize, or point fingers; your job is to pray.

Once again, it's not your issue; it should not affect your faith. Faith in God is an individual walk. You cannot enter heaven on your grandmother's, your mother's, or even your spouse's coattail. Do not be discouraged; this is what the enemy wants. This is also another tactic he uses to get people to doubt God's word. The thought is if pastors are committing the same types of sin as the world, then they are not believing the word they are preaching. If so, why should I? This may be on the hearts of many people, but it all comes down to your life in eternity. Eternity is real, and it is a great deal longer than your lifespan. Do you really want to back away from a future of peace to one of pain? The choice is yours. They've made a choice, and now, so do you.

The word of God says to mark the perfect man, which means to follow the pastor, minister, mentor, etc., who is allowing the word of God to become alive in him, and whose desire is to please God by inquiring of Him daily. In 2 Samuel 22:31 it says, "As for God, His way is perfect; the word of the Lord is tried: He is a buckler to all them that trust in Him." The human race is not perfect, but a person is made perfect when he or she follows God's *way*, which is perfect. God's way leads to life, and man's way leads to death. You cannot go wrong following God because His word has been tested and tried and He protects all who trust in Him. Hang in there; no one promised that this road would be easy. Remember, the Lord Jesus Christ is with you every step of the way on your life's journey. He will get you where He's promised to take you. Keep

> **You go to church not to "just do" church but to learn how to "be" the church!**

building your relationship with God by staying in His word, attending a good, Bible-based church weekly, and walking out (demonstrating) His principles in your life daily. As you continue to get God's word in your heart, it will transform you from the inside out. There will be a powerful change in your character; the real you will be transformed, and those who knew you before will see a difference in you. Sometimes they may try to take you back down memory lane and reminisce in order to recall your life before Christ, but you are no longer that person. You have been redeemed! Your sins have been forgiven, and you are now living the high life in Jesus. With God's word abiding in you and you abiding in His word, you are able to impact the lives of those around you. They will see God's love, peace, patience, joy, compassion, and generosity in you. You go to church not to "just do" church but to learn how to *be* the church!

Revelation from God

On June 9, 2015, I received a revelation from God concerning our love walk with Him. I discovered that we must love Him how He needs us to love Him at certain times in our relationship. The same is true with our natural relationships. You cannot love people the way you feel they need to be loved and expect them to receive it joyfully. No ... you must love them how they need to be loved in order for them to feel loved. Explaining it in the natural will help

> *You cannot love people the way "you feel" they need to be loved...you must love them "how" they need to be loved.*

you to see it in the spirit. As a husband and wife start their new journey together, the wife may need him to love her by demonstrating protection and provision. A new wife doesn't want to have to go back home to her parents or his parents for that matter because they cannot survive on their own. She needs him to provide for the home and to keep a roof over their heads, and he loves her by doing just that. He may work extra hours or even get a second job in order to keep the bills paid. Let us fast forward ten years.

At this stage in their relationship, she has the surety, but now she needs help with the kids. During the first years of their marriage, the wife knew that since her husband worked long hours she was responsible for the children. She fed them, bathed them, and even kept them away from Daddy to allow him to get some needed rest. She now needs him to help her with the kids. He's now working one job (9–5 p.m.), and she could definitely use some assistance. Her love now requests of him to step in and allow her to have a couple of hours to herself. This can be accomplished as he gets the children up on a Saturday morning and heads to McDonalds to get breakfast for the family. After breakfast, he then gets them to assist him in washing the car and they have a water day with the hose after that. She sees that he loves her through the meeting of her needs, and in return, she might even be an assistant to what he desires later.

As relationships develop and flourish, we must learn our mates so that we "know" what they need at each stage in order for the relationship to continue growing. The more we grow the more we should know about each other and their needs. Oftentimes we say that we're on the same page as our mate because we're finishing each other's sentences. This is a part of knowing your spouse. If your spouse is constantly repeating something or gets agitated easily about a topic, then the other mate needs to key in on this and show love by meeting this need. Love is not complicated, but it requires us to pay attention to our partner.

It is the same with our heavenly Father. We must be willing to love Him how He needs us to love Him at each stage in our relationship. Our Father knows where we are in our love walk, and He knows what is needed in order for us to continue growing in Christ. Sometimes we go through situations over and over again wondering why, but this could very well be God telling us that He needs us to love Him more in this area. Paying attention to our situations will help to alleviate extra time spent in the quandary. We may need to work on self-control and patience, and God maybe saying to us through situations, "Learn the lesson and pass the test so I can love you how you need to be loved at this time. I'm ready to answer your prayers, but you need to develop in this area so I can bless you as I have promised. I am ready to take you to another dimension in Me. Just pass the test."

Do you know that He is so ready to shower you with His blessings like never before? The word says that God desires you to prosper and be in health, even as your soul prospers. In other words, He wants you blessed in every area of your life! Do not get caught up in complaining and always asking, "Why me?" Get through the trial knowing that the testing of your faith works patience. James 1:4 says, "But let patience have her perfect work, that ye may be perfect and entire, wanting nothing."

He desires us to be all that He created us to be. Let us not despise the trial because it could be the vehicle God is using to bring increase in our lives. In the natural we understand the phrase, "No pain, no gain," and we continue because we know that in the end we'll have those great abs. Even more so, let's push through the pains of the trials that come against us and look toward the finish line because we know that our victory will be even greater than those abs!

Loving God how He needs us to love Him empowers us to develop our character, to mature spiritually, to manifest the fruits of the Spirit in our lives, to exude joy, to be strengthened, and to become more like Christ, ultimately bringing glory to His name. Truly loving someone requires both parties in the relationship to make the other person better—building them up. In the end, we are restored (confident, strong, and complete), and we represent God by having dominion and being His expression of love in the earth. This is what our Lord Jesus does for us. He knows what we need and is willing and able to do it but needs us to understand that we can tie His hands by not doing our part (submitting) in the relationship.

So let's begin handling our relationship with our Father in a more desirable way. Let's wake up in the morning asking God, "What can I do for You today?" Why? Because this shows that our hearts are set on pleasing Him and in return, guess what happens? As we delight ourselves in Him, it is His pleasure to give us the desires of our hearts. Wow!

It's His pleasure to give you the kingdom, to prosper you, and to cause you to walk into everything His word says is yours! In the natural, you can have the marriage and family that God says you can have because you are a winner in Christ and for you all things *are* possible. Just receive this revelation for yourself and begin to apply the principles thereof so you can have what God says you can have. He loves you. He wants the best for you. This is what true love accomplishes in Christ. God's kind of love is reciprocal. It causes you to bring out the best in someone else, and it causes them to bring out the best in you. Go on and get your blessing!

On Your Way

Beginning your new journey with God starts by building your relationship with Him. I encourage you to enter into it with great expectancy. Expect God to keep His word concerning His promises to you, and you expect to be changed by those very promises that you are applying to your life.

When you are expecting, you are looking forward to something—that's faith. The word of God says in Hebrews 11:6, "Now faith is the substance of things hoped for, the evidence of things not seen." It is going to take faith to please God. The word also says that He is a rewarder of them that diligently seek Him. He called you, He chose you, now allow Him to use you for His glory. He wants to reward you. This relationship will inevitably shape, form, and mold you into the *you* God has created you to be!

You've learned that in building your relationship with Him you must love, trust, agree, devote, submit, humble, ask every day, walk by the Spirit, and meditate and apply His word to your life. You've also seen how important it is to stay focused on this journey. There will be challenges, but nothing that you cannot handle as you continue to trust the Lord and not lean unto your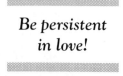

Be persistent in love!

own understanding. The Lord God said, "I will never leave you nor forsake you."

There is something that the Lord shared with me, and I want to share with you. It is this: be persistent in love! This is the key to building a relationship with Him.

We often sing about going back to Eden and living on top of the world—living blessed, at peace, and healed. Well, by operating in God's love we can because love conquers all. As we love others with the agape love of God, it destroys all types of yokes from our lives. God's love destroys hate, strife, jealousy, etc. Love is the most powerful force in the universe. It conquers lusts and temptations, it overcomes every obstacle in your life, and it stops every weapon that forms against you. Love satisfies your every need, and it causes you to be victorious! Walking out God's love begins with the mind. You must renew your mind by reading the word of God. Determine today that you will pursue love with everything within you, for as you do, you are on your way to doing great exploits for God!

In today's times, we must allow our light (love of Jesus) to shine brightly because the world around us is growing darker. People are becoming hopeless, their situations bleak, and their problems seem insurmountable, but we have the answer … Jesus. God needs us to operate in His love like never before. He does not desire that men perish but come to repentance. By being persistent in love, you are allowing God to work in you, with you, and through you so people can experience Him tangibly. The Lord Jesus wants to use you in the end time harvesting of souls. Someone had been praying for you, and now it's time for you to pray, encourage, and show compassion to the person God directs you to. You may not know all of the scriptures, but you do know what Jesus has done for you. This is what you share, and you will begin to see God open doors for you, fill your heart with words to say, and direct your path on things to do. Our Father is looking for those who will make themselves available to Him. Let Him use the tools He's given you: eyes to see the need of people; ears to hear their cry; a heart to have compassion; hands to assist them in their need; and a mouth to speak the words of God to break the chains and set them free.

I asked God for a nugget for the book one day while I was at the park walking around the track. Almost instantaneously, I received this revelation of the scripture—the race is not given to the swift, nor to the strong, but to him that endures. Here's my routine when I first starting working out. I walked six laps around the track, which equaled two miles. Then I began jogging a half lap on every other lap. I noticed my endurance increased when I jogged three-quarters of a lap. Then one day

I was jogging and reached the three-quarter mark, and I felt the Holy Spirit encouraging me to continue. I noticed that I wasn't as winded or tired at this point, so I continued. Before long, I had jogged one and a quarter lap. *Wow*, I said to myself. Then the Holy Spirit brought to my remembrance that we can do all things through Christ who strengthens us. Oftentimes we limit ourselves by not pushing ourselves. Let's give ourselves a fighting chance by not giving up and continuously moving forward.

We sometimes look at others who are stronger than we are and feel inadequate. You know, we even do this in the things of God. We'll see someone who is quick with knowing the scriptures or someone who prays with such power and intensity and think they are great. At that very moment, the enemy of our faith slips in and makes us feel that we will never reach that level, but he is a liar. Do not be jealous or envious, for this is *not* the spirit of God. No, use this to encourage yourself to press into the things of God. Remember, the reward is not given to the swift or strong but to him who endures to the end. It's given to him who loves in spite of; who trusts in spite of; who agrees with His word in spite of; who devotes his heart in spite of; who submits his will in spite of; who humbles himself in spite of; who asks every day in spite of; who meditates and applies the word of God in spite of; who walks by the Spirit in spite of; and who is persistent in pleasing Him in spite of present situations or circumstances.

Our Father is looking for a no-matter-what Christian! No matter what comes or goes, I am going to serve the Lord. This is him who receives the reward from God. Be not dismayed; God is not mocked. Whatsoever a man soweth, that shall he also reap. You sow to the spirit—love, trust, agreement,

> *Our Father is looking for a no-matter-what Christian!*

etc., to begin building a relationship with Him; then you shall reap of the spirit—joy, peace, favor, answered prayers, open doors, increase, prosperity, health, etc. You are on your way to building a genuine relationship with God!

Decision to Receive God's Forgiveness

I would like to take this time to thank you for reading *I'm Saved …
What's Next?* Most people who have read this book are saved, but just
in case if you are not, I pray that it has inspired you to make a decision
today to choose the Lord and begin building a relationship with Him.
If you were once saved, but somehow lost your way, now is the perfect
time to rededicate yourself to the Lord. He loves you and has never given
up on you!

Regardless of whether this is your first time receiving our Father's
forgiveness or not, receiving Jesus as your personal Savior and Lord of
your life is the best decision you will ever make. Romans 10:9 says that if
you confess with your mouth that Jesus is Lord and believe in your heart
that God has raised Him from the dead, you will be saved. It is simple
to do; just pray this prayer aloud with a sincere heart:

Father God, You are the One who created the heavens and the earth
and me, too. I am a sinner who is separated from You by my sins. My
lifestyle has been against all that You believe in. Thank You for giving
Your Son, Jesus, as ransom for me. I believe that He died, was buried,
was resurrected, and now sits at Your right hand praying for me. I repent
of my sins, and I receive Your way of forgiveness. I receive Jesus as my
Savior and the Lord of my life. Father, baptize me with Your Holy Spirit,
and fill me to overflowing with the evidence of speaking in tongues. I
want all that You have for me so I can live my life holy and pleasing
before You. Thank You for receiving me into Your family. I am Yours
and You are mine. Teach me how to live my life for You starting today
in Jesus's name. Amen.

You have now become a child of the Most High God! You may not feel any different, but just know that you have been translated from darkness into His marvelous light. That means you have gone from death to life, just like that! Your next step is to find a local-Bible teaching church where you can learn and grow in the word of God. Also, begin participating in an area of ministry to help support the work of the Lord. This will assist you with leadership skills and to nurture the gifts and talents God has placed in you to benefit others. You are here to serve. The word of God says that it is more blessed to give than receive. You'll experience the joy of blessing others. Get excited because God's work in you has just begun. The best is yet to come. Always remember to share the "good news" (Jesus saves) with someone because you are truly blessed to be a blessing!

I pray that God will surround you with people who will support and encourage you on your journey with Christ. May God's angels encamp around you daily to minister, guard and protect, and battle for you in the heavens. I also pray God's guidance, favor, and peace be upon you daily. It's my prayer that you will continue moving forward with all vigor in your relationship with Christ. You are now walking with God and walking in the *right* direction! May God bless and keep you is my prayer. Welcome to the family, my brother or sister in Christ!

Encouragement Just for You

From One Family Member to Another

You are God's child. You now belong to Him. He is your God. He is your friend; therefore, trust Him to lead you today and every day. He loves you like no one else. This journey may not be easy at times, but just know that He is always with you. You are His beloved, and He is here to protect you from evil. Just trust Him with all that you have. Remember, it was He who has allowed you to have it. He wants to lavish His love upon you. He wants to share His innermost thoughts with you. God wants to keep you from all hurt and harm. You are His beloved.

One day you will meet Him face-to-face, and it's His desire to say to you, "Enter into my rest, my good and faithful servant." So, remember to keep yourself away from those things that would appear evil, those things that will try to turn your heart back to the ways of your past, and those things that will try to make you doubt Him. His word is true. You can count on Him. He will never fail you. He cannot lie. Whatever He says is true. You are His disciple, you are His friend, and you are His child, so hold fast to His word in you. It will keep you. It will comfort you. It will bring encouragement to you. How, you might ask? Because it's Him whispering to you the plans that He has for you. Just listen carefully. You can hear Him. He is always speaking to you. He is always entreating you. He is always longing for you because He loves you. Rest in Him today and always. He loves you deeply.

Blessings upon you,
Brenda

Printed in the United States
by Baker & Taylor Publisher Services